AF599187

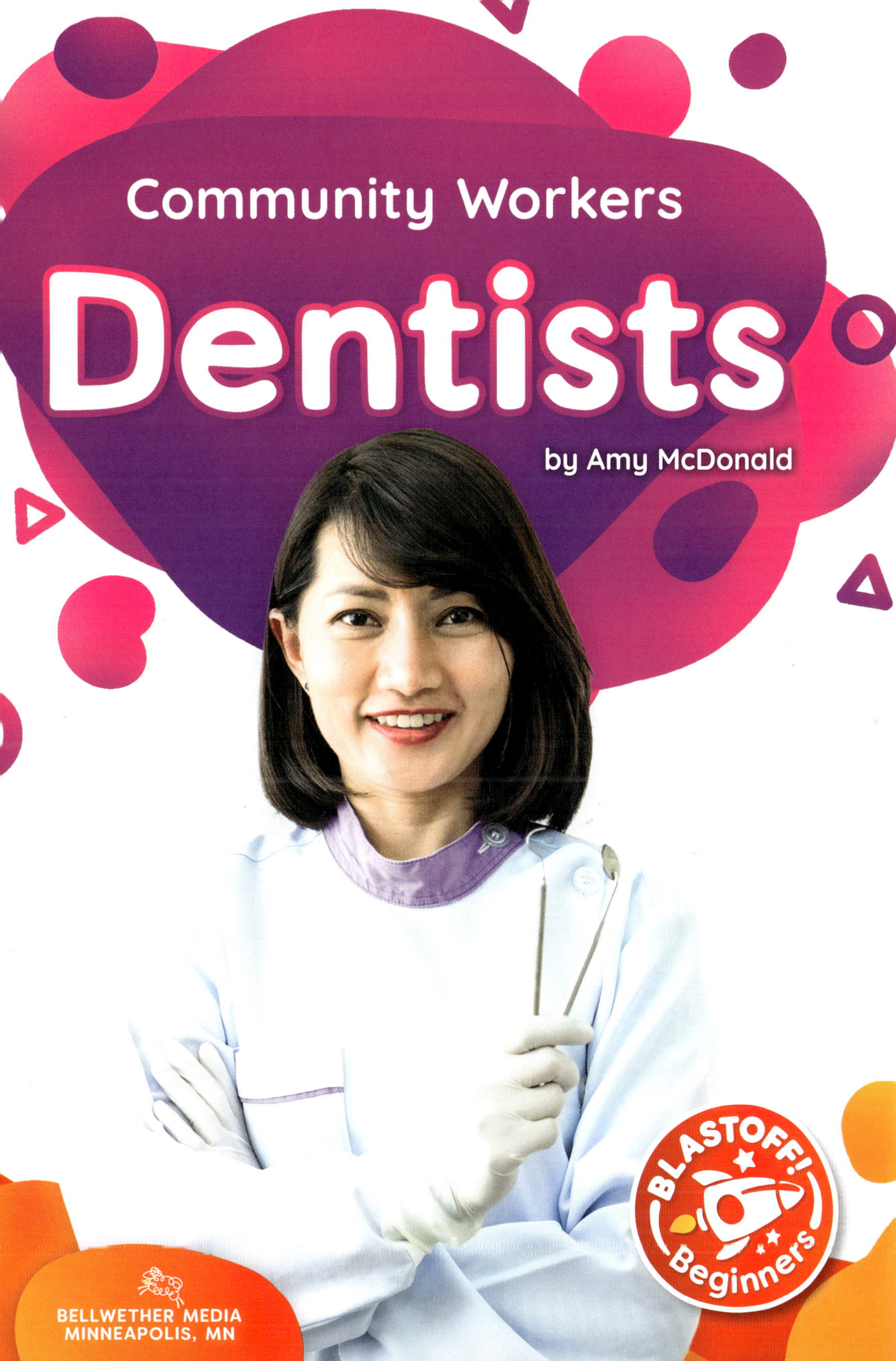
Community Workers
Dentists
by Amy McDonald
BLASTOFF!
Beginners
BELLWETHER MEDIA
MINNEAPOLIS, MN

Blastoff! Beginners are developed by literacy experts and educators to meet the needs of early readers. These engaging informational texts support young children as they begin reading about their world. Through simple language and high frequency words paired with crisp, colorful photos, Blastoff! Beginners launch young readers into the universe of independent reading.

Sight Words in This Book

and	is	to
are	look	use
for	of	
have	the	
here	them	
how	they	

This edition first published in 2025 by Bellwether Media, Inc.

Library of Congress Cataloging-in-Publication Data

LC record for Dentists available at: https://lccn.loc.gov/2024004951

Editor: Betsy Rathburn Designer: Laura Sowers

Printed in the United States of America, North Mankato, MN.

Table of Contents

On the Job

Smile!
The dentist
is here.

What Are They?

Dentists are doctors.
They care for teeth and gums.

They have chairs.
They use tools.

What Do They Do?

Dentists clean teeth. They use **picks**. They use **floss**.

pick

They check gums.
They use **mirrors**.

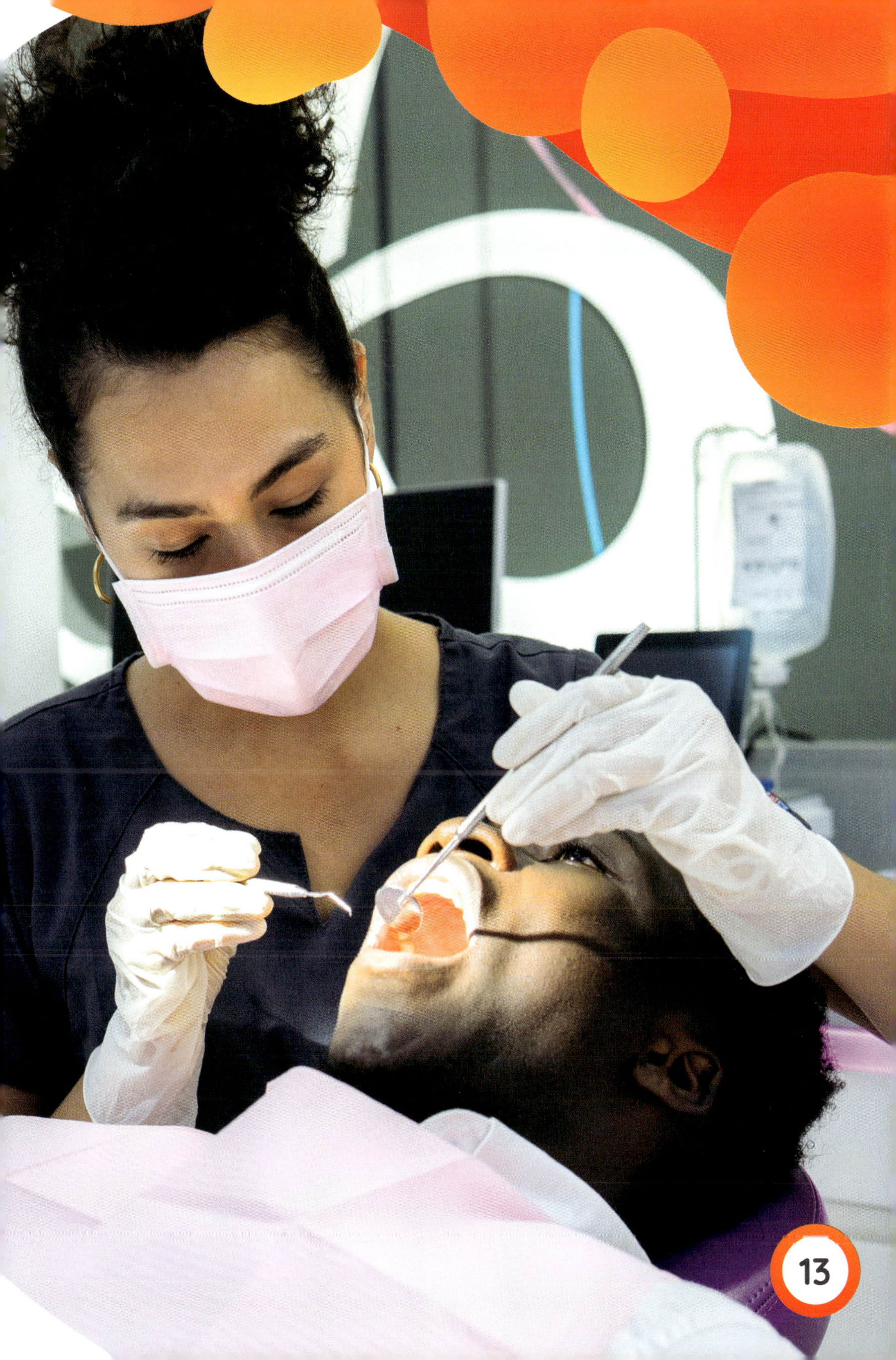

They take pictures of teeth. They look for problems.

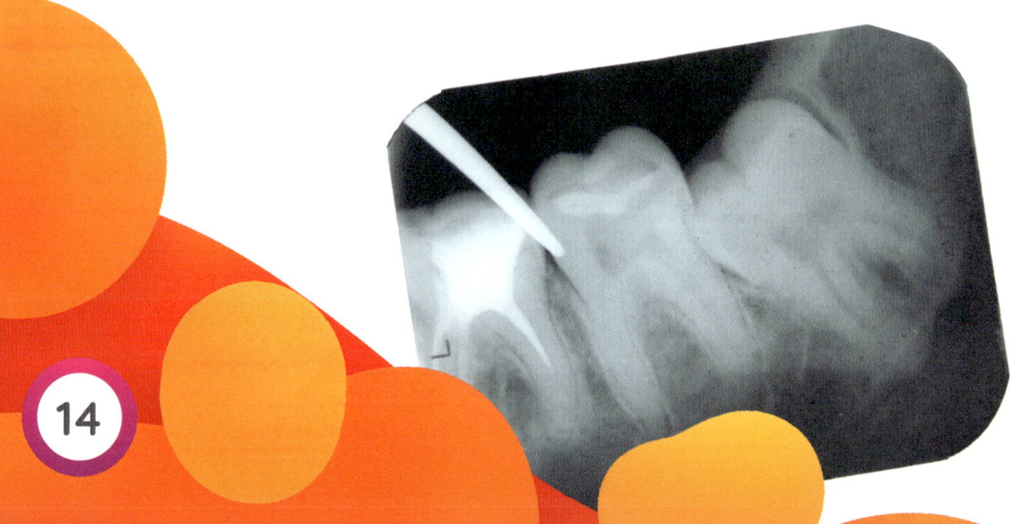

They fix
broken teeth.

They give toothbrushes. They show how to use them.

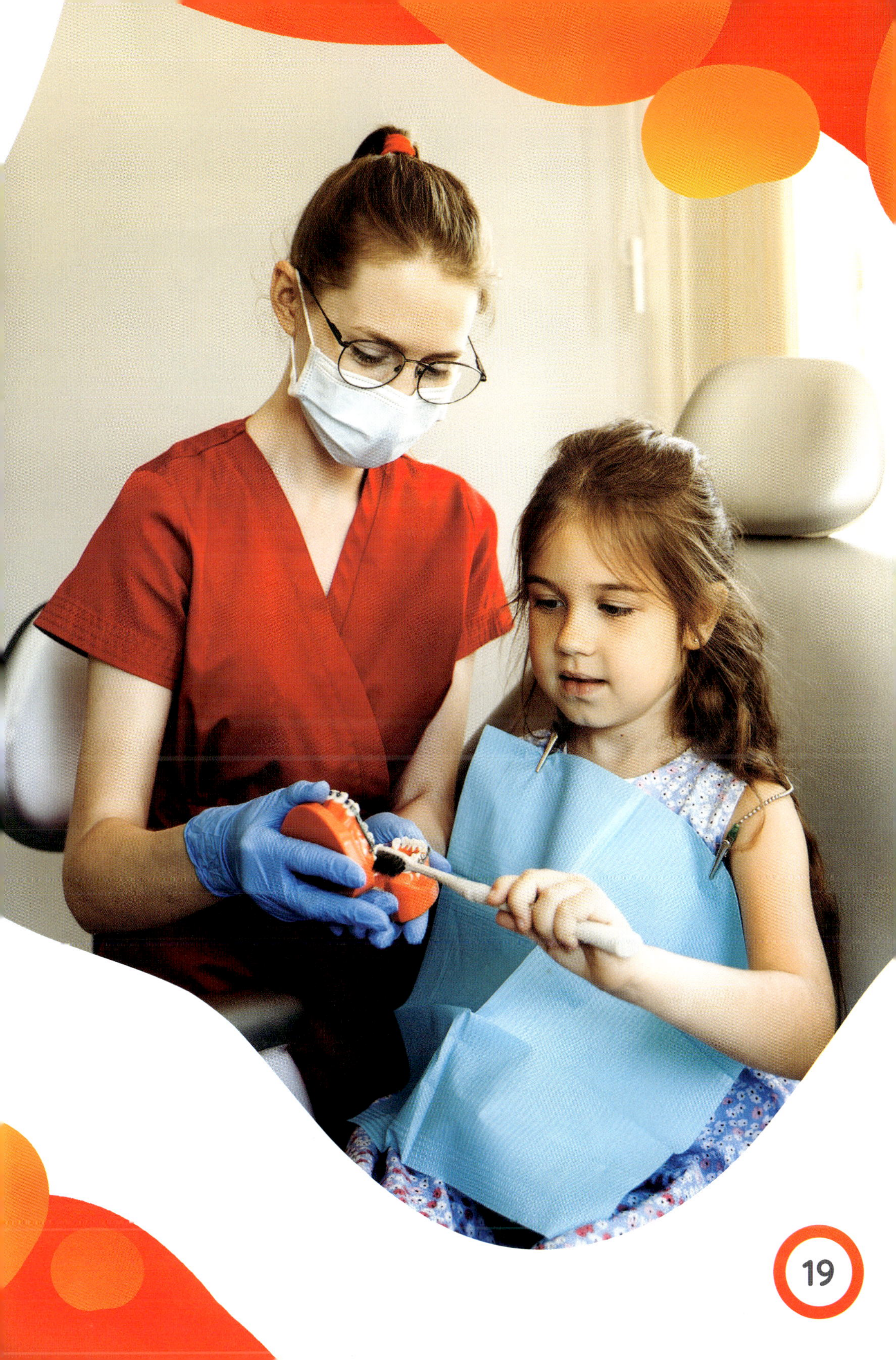

Why Do We Need Them?

Dentists give us healthy smiles!

Dentist Facts

Tools

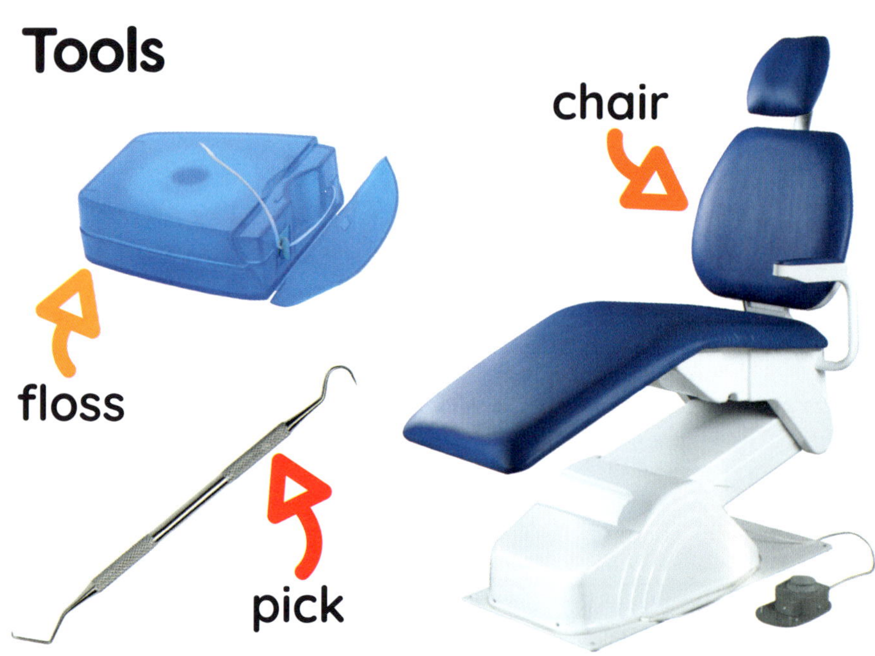

A Day in the Life

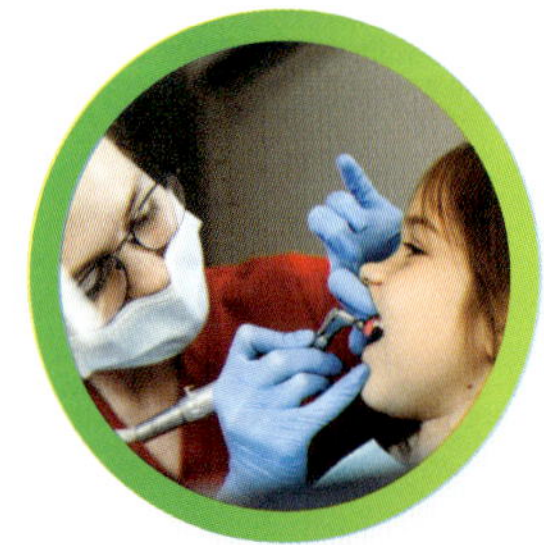

clean teeth

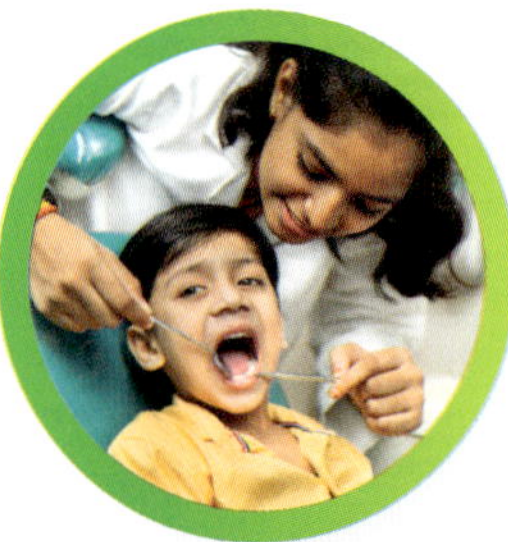

check gums

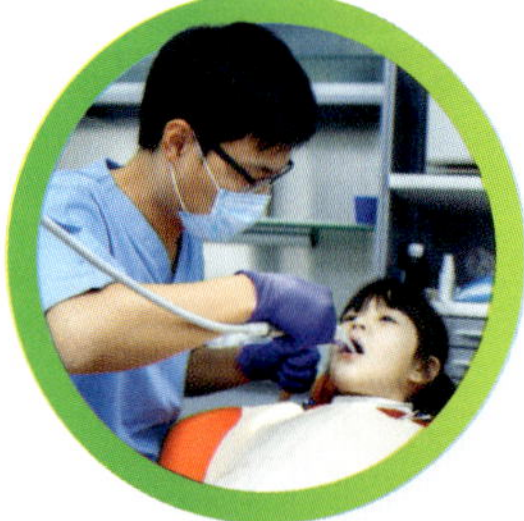

fix broken teeth

Glossary

floss

string used to clean between teeth

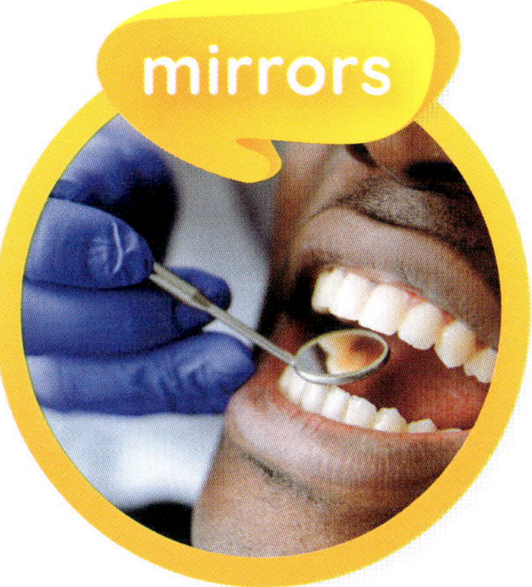

mirrors

tools that help dentists see inside mouths

picks

tools with a sharp point

To Learn More

ON THE WEB

FACTSURFER

Factsurfer.com gives you a safe, fun way to find more information.

1. Go to www.factsurfer.com.
2. Enter "dentists" into the search box and click 🔍.
3. Select your book cover to see a list of related content.

Index

The images in this book are reproduced through the courtesy of: worawit_j, front cover; JoanneStrell, p. 3; SeventyFour, pp. 4-5; Monkey Business Images, pp. 6-7; Anton Starikov, p. 8 (tools); Drazen Zigic, pp. 8-9; Luis Carlos Torres, p. 10 (floss); RusAKphoto, pp. 10-11; HASSOLDBOY, p. 12 (mirror); ADDICTIVE STOCK CREATIVES/ Alamy, pp. 12-13; Aliaksandr Barouski, pp. 14, 16-17; Roman Chazov, pp. 14-15; Dicky Algofari, p. 18 (toothbrush); Rabizo Anatolii, pp. 18-19, 22 (clean teeth); Gelpi, p. 20; Geber86, pp. 20-21; igra.design, p. 22 (floss); s-ts, p. 22 (pick); Denis Polikarpov, p. 22 (chair); Clovera, p. 22 (check gums); Flotsam, p. 22 (fix broken teeth); Vershinin89, p. 23 (floss); V_Lisovoy, p. 23 (mirrors); Milanmarkovic, p. 23 (picks).